Lucky Duck is more than a publishing house and training agency. George Robinson and Barbara Maines founded the company in the 1980s when they worked together as a head and as a psychologist, developing innovative strategies to support challenging students.

They have an international reputation for their work on bullying, self-esteem, emotional literacy and many other subjects of interest to the world of education.

George and Barbara have set up a regular news-spot on the website at http://www.luckyduck.co.uk/newsAndEvents/viewNewsItems and information about their training programmes can be found at www.insetdays.com

More details about Lucky Duck can be found at http://www.luckyduck.co.uk/

Visit the website for all our latest publications in our specialist topics

- Emotional Literacy
- Bullying
- Circle Time
- Asperger's Syndrome
- Self-esteem
- Positive Behaviour Management
- Anger Management
- Eating Disorders

Mighty Motivators

A resource bank for setting targets and
rewarding pupil progress for 5 to 11 year olds

Claire Moore and Tina Rae

Illustrated by Tina Rae

P·C·P
Paul Chapman
Publishing

ISBN: 1-4129-1075-7

Published by Lucky Duck
⚜ Paul Chapman Publishing
A SAGE Publications Company
1 Oliver's Yard
55 City Road
London EC1Y 1SP

SAGE Publications, Inc.
2455 Teller Road
Thousand Oaks, California 91320

SAGE Publications India Pvt Ltd
B-42, Panchsheel Enclave
Post Box 4109
New Delhi 110 017

www.luckyduck.co.uk

Commissioning Editors: George Robinson and Barbara Maines
Editorial Team: Mel Maines, Wendy Ogden and Sarah Lynch
Illustrator: Tina Rae
Designer: Helen Weller

© Claire Moore and Tina Rae 2005

Printed and bound by Cromwell Press, Trowbridge, Wiltshire

Contents

Introduction and Background   7

Bibliography   10

The Aims of the Resource Bank   11

The Structure of the Resource Bank   12

Section 1   Target Book Front Covers   15

Section 2   Daily Reward Colouring Sheets   21

Section 3   Daily Reward Collection Sheets   27

Section 4   Weekly Reward Charts   33

Section 5   More Specific Weekly Reward Charts   39

Section 6   Playtime Reward Charts   45

Section 7   Reward Charts for School and Home Comments   51

Section 8   Sticker Sheets   57

Section 9   Certificates for School and Home   63

Section 10   Reward Badges   69

Section 11   Bookmark Rewards   73

Section 12   Achievement Cards   77

How to use the CD-ROM

The CD-ROM contains PDF files, clearly labelled to correspond to each relevant section. You will need Acrobat Reader version 3 or higher to view and print these resources.

The documents are set up to print to A4 but you can enlarge them to A3 by increasing the output percentage at the point of printing using the page set-up settings for your printer.

A Note on Key Stages

Key Stage 1 covers the ages 5 to 7.

Key Stage 2 covers the ages 7 to 11.

Introduction and Background

This resource bank has been developed for use in infant and primary schools and aims to provide teachers, children and parents/carers with a range of attractive materials and ideas which will promote self-esteem and positive behaviour and encourage effective target setting for both behaviour management and learning.

Target setting in schools 'has been shown in research and inspection evidence to help raise standards of pupil performance' (DfEE circular 11/98) and the Government is consequently committed to supporting such a process via appropriate levels of funding and guidance and a new legal requirement. Alongside a range of statutory targets such as those for Literacy and Numeracy, schools may also take the opportunity to set targets in other areas. Such additional targets 'may be especially relevant to pupils with Special Needs or high ability' and schools may also opt to publish targets in areas such as social and personal development (DfEE circular 11/98). However this process should not be seen as merely a statistical record but rather as 'a powerful way for schools to set clear and direct goals for raising standards' (Hopkins and Harris 1998). Specific personal targets that may relate to the development of confidence and self-esteem, and may consequently be non-numerical, are also central to the teaching and learning relationship. Finding appropriate ways to cut through the barriers to learning, whether these are emotional ('within child') or curriculum based ('outside child') is an essential objective for teachers, who need to ensure the inclusion and development of all children in their care.

These resources aim to encourage teachers, parents or carers, and children to work in partnership in setting a range of appropriate targets, which will promote positive attitudes to learning and behaviour within the classroom and school context. Children will be encouraged to see themselves as learners in a positive way. This will enhance their self-image and in turn affect their learning and behaviour. This has been found to be particularly successful in reinforcing 'the value of positive emotions in learning' (Cartwright and Dehaney 2000) and in developing the link between children's emotional wellbeing and successful learning behaviours.

The resources can be used to reinforce positive learning patterns and behaviours in all children, but we have utilised them to the greatest effect with children who exhibit learning and emotional and behavioural difficulties.

An Inclusive Approach

The SEN Code of Practice on the Identification and Assessment of pupils with Special Educational Needs (DfEE 2000) emphasises the critical role that parents play in their children's education:

'There are strong reasons for working in partnership with all parents. If they feel confident that schools and professionals actively involve them, take account of their wishes, feelings and unique perspectives on their children's development, then the work of those schools and professionals can be more effective' (DfEE 2000, page 9).

This document also reinforces the rights of the child, referring to articles 12, 13 and 23 of the United Nations Convention on the Rights of the Child, adopted by the United Nations General Assembly in 1989 and ratified by the United Kingdom in 1991. These articles detail how children have a right to obtain and make known information, to express an opinion, and to have that opinion taken into account in any matter or procedure affecting the child. The Code of Practice demands that pupil participation should be the goal for all children and states that 'children with Special Educational Needs should be actively involved at an appropriate level in discussions about their Individual Education Plans (IEPs), any target setting and review arrangements, and have those views recorded' (DfEE 2000, page 16).

This resource bank is designed to encourage parents/carers, teachers and children to work together in order to identify and formulate targets and to agree reward systems and strategies, which will help the child to meet the targets set. When devising any type of individual behaviour or learning plan, the teacher will need to work directly with the parents and child from the outset. Without such collaboration from the start, any such programme will be less effective. Setting agreed and appropriate targets, choosing target books, reward sheets or charts, and agreeing rewards and review arrangements for the individual child all need to be done via a meeting with all people involved.

The Code of Practice highlights the importance of such involvement, particularly for those children with Special Educational Needs who may have low self-esteem and who lack confidence: 'Actively encouraging these pupils to track their own progress and record achievement within a programme of action designed to meet their particular learning or behavioural difficulty will contribute to improved confidence and self-image (DfEE 2000, pages 16–17).

Making use of these resources in such a way should aid progress in target areas alongside contributing to the further improvement of children's confidence and self-esteem.

Motivating the Child with Emotional and Behavioural Difficulties

Children may experience behavioural difficulties for a variety of reasons, including family stress, medical needs, peer pressure or problems and bereavement. However, the most important cause of such difficulties is to be found in low self-esteem and the failure of those who care for the children to provide consistent, nurturing boundaries and positive reinforcement.

When we focus upon children's apparent difficulties or failures, we are most likely to damage their self-esteem and consequently have a negative effect upon their development and attainment. Making use of positive behaviour management strategies such as reinforcing appropriate behaviours, celebrating successes, and giving praise, time and special approval are more likely to positively influence progress and development.

Teachers can play a significant role in this process as they are in the most unique, special and powerful position in terms of contributing to the child's development on a daily basis. They are able to raise self-esteem by:

▸ Providing appropriately differentiated tasks and work that protects children from failure.

▸ Including activities that promote emotional literacy and social skills within the curriculum.

▸ Designing activities that are engaging and promote a sense of genuine achievement on completion.

▸ Breaking tasks down into shorter, achievable chunks that can then be further extended as the child's skills and competencies increase.

▸ Making use of a positive marking policy.

▸ Adopting good practice in terms of classroom management and organisation i.e. a sensitive approach to seating arrangements, lining up and other daily routines.

▸ Giving genuine praise and positive reinforcement on a daily basis.

▸ Modelling and reinforcing appropriate social and emotional behaviours, and providing children with opportunities to practise these skills.

▸ Sharing and reinforcing individual children's successes with the peer group and parents.

▸ Empowering children by involving them in decision-making and giving them responsibilities.

▸ Continually 'catching them being good' and rewarding appropriate behaviours as soon as they occur.

This last strategy is probably one of the simplest and most practical ways of helping children to behave well and to learn effectively within the classroom.

These resources consequently reflect this fact, providing a variety of formats to encourage personal target setting and to reward children's successes and achievements.

Bibliography

Burns, M. and Saunders, L. (1999) *Target Setting: From Policy to Practice.* 'Topic' Issue 22.

Cartwright, T. and Dehaney, R.(2000) Safety Netting Your Classroom. *Special Children* Issue 132. Questions Publishing.

Cooper, P. (1993) *Effective Schools for Disaffected Students.* Routledge. London.

Cooper, P. (ed) (1995) *Helping Them to Learn Curriculum Entitlement for Children with Emotional and Behavioural difficulties.* NASEN.

Curry, M. and Branfield, C.(1994) *Personal and Social Education for Primary Schools Through Circle Time.* NASEN.

DfEE Circular 10/99 Social Inclusion: *Pupil Support.*

DfEE Circular 11/98 *Target Setting in Schools.*

DfEE (1993) *Pupil Behaviour and Discipline.*

DfEE (1993) *The Education of Children With Emotional and Behavioural Difficulties.*

DfEE (2000) *The Code of Practice on the Identification and Assessment of Pupils with Special Educational Needs.*

Elton Report (1989) A report commissioned by the government to address the issue of behaviour management in a positive and planned way.

Galvin, P. Mercer, S. and Costa, P. (1990) *Building a Better Behaved School.* Longman

Gordan, R. (1996) *The Primary Behaviour File.* PfP, London.

HMSO *Discipline in Schools*, Report of the Committee of Enquiry Chaired by Lord Elton.

Hopkins, D. and Harris, A. (1998) Improving City Schools: The Role of the LEA.

Education Journal, December 1998, pages 22-23.

Luton, K. Booth, G. Leadbetter, J. Tee, G. and Wallace, F. (1991) *Positive Strategies for Behaviour Management.* NFER Nelson.

Moore, C and Rae, T (2000) *Positive People. A Self Esteem Building Course for Young Children.* Lucky Duck Publishing Ltd. Bristol.

Robinson, G., Maines, B. (1995) *Celebrations.* Lucky Duck Publishing Ltd. Bristol

Warden, D. and Christie, D. (1997) *Teaching Social Behaviour.* David Fulton Publishers.

The Aims of the Resource Bank

In making use of the resources in *Mighty Motivators*, teachers will be aiming to ensure the following:

▸ To include children and their parents or carers in the target setting, reward and review processes, in order to develop a united and consistent approach between school and home.

▸ To further increase children's self-esteem and self-worth and ensure that children experience what it is to feel good about themselves.

▸ For children, parents and teachers to recognise, articulate and record positive achievements.

▸ To particularly encourage children to become reflective and to think about their behaviour, achievements and learning style, to consider how and when they can make progress and identify who can help them in this process.

▸ To empower children by involving them in decisions about their individual programmes.

▸ For teachers and parents to focus on the positives and to continually reward appropriate behaviours, effort and achievements as soon as they occur.

▸ That teachers become more reflective regarding their own practice in terms of motivating children to learn and behave appropriately in the school context.

▸ That targets are set which protect the children from failure, i.e. SMART targets, which are Specific, Measurable, Achievable, Realistic and Time-bound.

▸ To further improve self-knowledge and the ability to accurately assess and celebrate progress.

▸ That teachers particularly consider and adopt good practice in terms of motivating all children to learn and behave appropriately, and that this practice is clearly articulated within the relevant school policy documents, including those covering behaviour, Special Educational Needs and teaching and learning.

The Structure of the Resource Bank

The resources can be printed from the CD-ROM. They are divided into 12 sections and are organised as follows:

Section 1: Target Books Front Covers.

A variety of front covers for Target books, with one design available for each reward sheet or chart.

Section 2: Daily Reward Colouring Sheets.

Daily reward sheets to be coloured in until the child reaches their target.

Section 3: Daily Reward Collection Sheets.

Daily reward sheets to collect mini-stickers or dots when the child reaches their target.

Section 4: Weekly Reward Charts.

Weekly reward sheets to colour or collect mini-stickers or dots, with an overview of the week.

Section 5: More Specific Weekly Reward Charts.

Weekly reward charts to collect mini-stickers or points, in a variety of formats.

Section 6: Playtime Reward Charts.

Playtime reward charts to collect mini-stickers or points, for rewarding appropriate behaviour.

Section 7: Reward Charts for School and Home Comments.

Weekly and playtime reward charts with space for school and home comments.

Section 8: Sticker Sheets.

Mini-illustrations for making into sticker rewards for children.

Section 9: Certificates for School and Home.

A variety of certificates for rewarding children's progress and celebrating with at home.

Section 10: Reward Badges.

Mini-designs for making into reward badges for children to wear with pride.

Section 11: Bookmark Rewards.

A variety of illustrated, useful bookmarks for rewarding children's achievements.

Section 12: Achievement Cards.

Reward cards for collecting points, marks, mini-stickers or dots in a handy format.

Building on Success and Looking Forward

The Elton Report, commissioned by the government in 1989, concluded that there should be a healthy balance between rewards and sanctions in schools, with both being clearly specified. It emphasised that in order to increase appropriate behaviour, teachers should reward it when it occurs, as is also the case with learning, effort, concentration, etc. This bank of resources is a starting point for doing exactly that.

These materials have been developed and made use of with individual children in infant and primary schools and have been found to be highly successful in developing children's personal awareness of their behaviours and learning through an inclusive approach, working collaboratively with the child and parents. This has subsequently been found to have positive influences on behaviours in the classroom and school contexts, as well as developing the self-esteem and confidence of many vulnerable children. It has helped children to value their successes and efforts in a positive and celebrated way, and has supported the increase in appropriate social and learning behaviours.

This resource bank provides many of the materials that teachers, children and parents may require in order to formulate complete individual learning or behaviour programmes and plans. There is an extensive range of attractive printable resources, which can form the initial basis for a Target Setting and Reward System within the school as a whole. There is the option for the busy teacher to choose a format with the child and parent that can then be quickly printed and personalised. There are further options to also design original Target books and reward charts using the blank formats provided, and for teachers to design and develop their own range of resources relevant to the interests and needs of the children in their care.

Most importantly, if access to these materials helps ensure an inclusive approach which further builds the self-esteem, confidence and skills of the children, alongside prompting staff to further consider and develop best practice in this area, then we feel that this publication will have been very worthwhile.

Section 1: Target Book Front Covers

Once the child has been identified as requiring an individualised learning or behaviour programme, specific targets, strategies and resources will need to be agreed with the child and parents/carers at an initial meeting.

A Target Book can then be made up and personalised for the child. It will be necessary to consider the specific interests of the child and for these to be reflected in the choice of Front Cover. Children can choose from the resources in this section or make use of the blank formats if they wish to design their own Front Cover.

We would strongly recommend making use of an A4 hole punched folder or file made from reasonably strong thin card, or an A4 exercise book onto which the chosen Front Cover can be glued. The child can then decorate the Front Cover using colouring pencils, felt tips or other drawing media in order to personalise it, ensuring that they include their name and the date when the Target Book was started. It is advisable to cover the folder or exercise book in sticky back plastic in order to maintain good presentation and increase durability.

This can then be used to store the daily and weekly reward sheets or charts in this resource bank or the personalised formats using the blank sheets at the end of each section.

My Target Book

Name ....
Date started ....

My Target Book

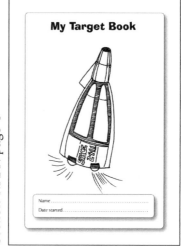

Name ....
Date started ....

My Target Book

Name ....
Date started ....

My Target Book

Name ....
Date started ....

My Target Book

Name ....
Date started ....

My Target Book

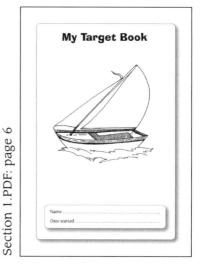

Name ....
Date started ....

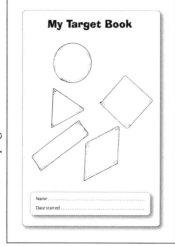

Section 1.PDF: page 7

My Target Book

Name ....
Date started ....

Section 1.PDF: page 8

My Target Book

Name ....
Date started ....

Section 1.PDF: page 9

My Target Book

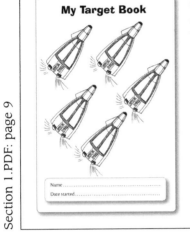

Name ....
Date started ....

Section 1.PDF: page 10

My Target Book

Name ....
Date started ....

Section 1.PDF: page 11

My Target Book

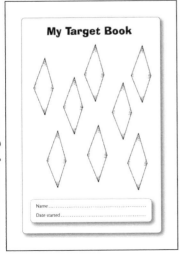

Name ....
Date started ....

Section 1.PDF: page 12

My Target Book

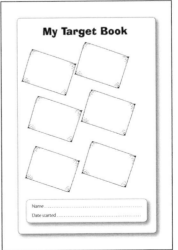

Name ....
Date started ....

My Target Book

Name ....
Date started ....

My Target Book

Name ....
Date started ....

My Target Book

Name ....
Date started ....

My Target Book

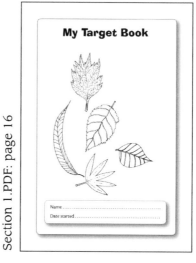

Name ....
Date started ....

My Target Book

Name ....
Date started ....

My Target Book

Name ....
Date started ....

18

My Target Book

Name ....
Date started ....

My Target Book

Name ....
Date started ....

My Target Book

WATER

Name ....
Date started ....

My Target Book

Name ....
Date started ....

My Target Book

Name ....
Date started ....

My Target Book

Name ....
Date started ....

Section 1.PDF: page 25

My Target Book

Name ....

Date started ....

Section 1.PDF: page 26

My Target Book

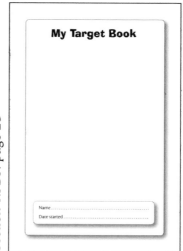

Name ....

Date started ....

Section 2: Daily Reward Colouring Sheets

For younger children, in particular, we have found it practical to make use of Daily Reward Sheets that allow for continual reinforcement of the set target and desired behaviours. Every time the teacher catches the child 'being good' or meeting the set target the child can then be directed to colour in the next part of the Daily Reward Sheet in sequence. If all the parts are coloured by the end of the day the child can receive a special sticker, reward or certificate to take home (as agreed at the initial meeting with parents).

A new Daily Reward Sheet will be used each day and selected targets may be continued and reinforced on a daily basis or adapted in the light of the child's response and progress.

The teacher will need to ensure that the child receives appropriate levels of reinforcement and praise throughout the day and will need to be vigilant in terms of observing that the specific target is being met. Encouraging the child to colour in the chart also allows the child to be more actively involved in the reward process and to often stop for a minute in order to reflect on the progress made.

The completed Reward Sheet can be shown to parents at the end of the day or a copy could be sent home. Alternatively feedback can be given to parents on the telephone on a daily or weekly basis, depending on which is most convenient for all those involved.

Example:

Name........ James ....

Date started ..12th October 2005 ....

Target........ I will sit next to my teacher ....

.... on the carpet. ....

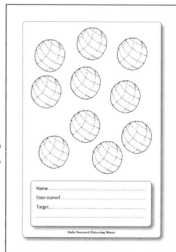

Name ....
Date started ....
Target ....
....
Daily Reward Colouring Sheet

Name ....
Date started ....
Target ....
....
Daily Reward Colouring Sheet

Section 2.PDF: page 3

Name ....
Date started ....
Target...
....
Daily Reward Colouring Sheet

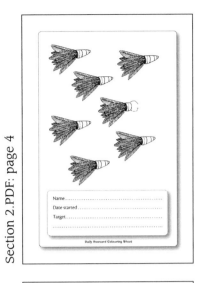

Section 2.PDF: page 4

Name ....
Date started ....
Target...
....
Daily Reward Colouring Sheet

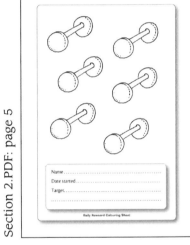

Section 2.PDF: page 5

Name ....
Date started ....
Target...
....
Daily Reward Colouring Sheet

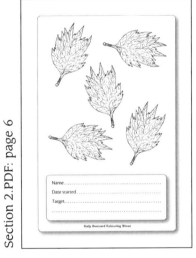

Section 2.PDF: page 6

Name ....
Date started ....
Target...
....
Daily Reward Colouring Sheet

Section 2.PDF: page 7

Name ....
Date started ....
Target...
....
Daily Reward Colouring Sheet

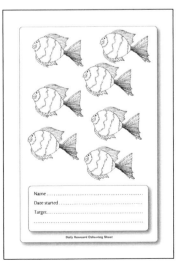

Section 2.PDF: page 8

Name ....
Date started ....
Target...
....
Daily Reward Colouring Sheet

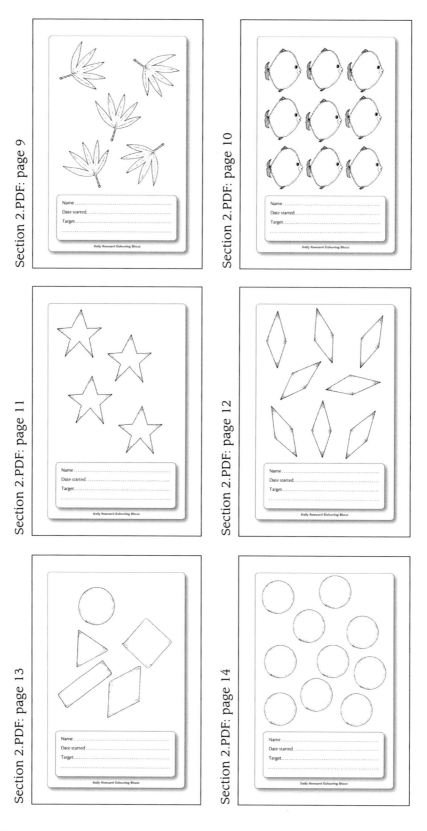

Section 2.PDF: page 9

Section 2.PDF: page 10

Section 2.PDF: page 11

Section 2.PDF: page 12

Section 2.PDF: page 13

Section 2.PDF: page 14

Name..
Date started...
Target..
....

Daily Rewcard Colouring Sheet

Name..
Date started...
Target..
....

Daily Rewcard Colouring Sheet

Name..
Date started...
Target..
....

Daily Rewcard Colouring Sheet

Name..
Date started...
Target..
....

Daily Rewcard Colouring Sheet

Name..
Date started...
Target..
....

Daily Rewcard Colouring Sheet

Name..
Date started...
Target..
....

Daily Rewcard Colouring Sheet

Section 2.PDF: page 21

Name ....
Date started ....
Target...
....

Daily Reward Colouring Sheet

Section 2.PDF: page 22

Name ....
Date started ....
Target...
....

Daily Reward Colouring Sheet

Section 2.PDF: page 23

Name ....
Date started ....
Target...
....

Daily Reward Colouring Sheet

Section 2.PDF: page 24

Name ....
Date started ....
Target...
....

Daily Reward Colouring Sheet

Section 2.PDF: page 25

Name ....
Date started ....
Target...
....

Daily Reward Colouring Sheet

Section 2.PDF: page 26

Name ....
Date started ....
Target...
....

Daily Reward Colouring Sheet

Section 3: Daily Reward Collection Sheets

As with the Daily Reward Colouring Sheets, we have also found these Daily Reward Collection Sheets to be particularly appropriate for younger children. However, rather than colouring in parts of the chart in sequence, the child can have access to a sheet of self-adhesive dots or mini-stickers which they can stick onto the chart as directed by the teacher. A strip of ten can be cut off and made readily available on a daily basis. These Reward Sheets are suitable for use in rewarding playtime and classroom behaviours, and learning targets. Teachers may wish to use different coloured dots to reward the child at different times in the day, for example, red for the morning session and blue for the afternoon, as this will then allow them to monitor times of the day in which the child experiences most success in meeting their target. This may subsequently help to inform future target setting which is relevant to the child's needs.

Again, encouraging the child to place his or her own 'reward' dots or mini-stickers onto the chart allows active involvement in the process. It also allows the child to reflect upon and reinforce the progress being made in meeting their target.

The completed Reward Sheet can be shown to parents/carers at the end of the day or a copy could be sent home. Alternatively feedback can be given to parents on the telephone on a daily or weekly basis, depending on which is most convenient for all those involved.

Examples:

Name........ Katharine
Date started.. 10th October 2005
Target........ I will stay in my chair and
work for at least 10 minutes.

Name........ Yusuf
Date started.. 10th October 2005
Target........ I will put my hand up when
I want to speak.

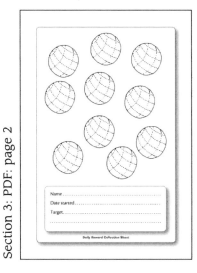

Section 3.PDF: page 3

Name ....
Date started ....
Target ....
....

Daily Reward Collection Sheet

Section 3.PDF: page 4

Name ....
Date started ....
Target ....
....

Daily Reward Collection Sheet

Section 3.PDF: page 5

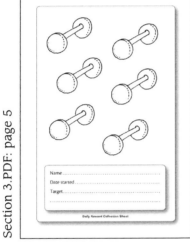

Name ....
Date started ....
Target ....
....

Daily Reward Collection Sheet

Section 3.PDF: page 6

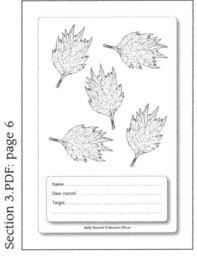

Name ....
Date started ....
Target ....
....

Daily Reward Collection Sheet

Section 3.PDF: page 7

Name ....
Date started ....
Target ....
....

Daily Reward Collection Sheet

Section 3.PDF: page 8

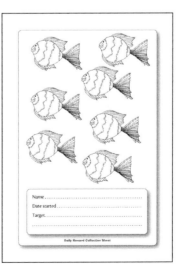

Name ....
Date started ....
Target ....
....

Daily Reward Collection Sheet

Section 3.PDF: page 15

Name . . . .
Date started . . . .
Target . . . .
. . . .

Daily Reward Collection Sheet

Section 3.PDF: page 16

Name . . . .
Date started . . . .
Target . . . .
. . . .

Daily Reward Collection Sheet

Section 3.PDF: page 17

Name . . . .
Date started . . . .
Target . . . .
. . . .

Daily Reward Collection Sheet

Section 3.PDF: page 18

Name . . . .
Date started . . . .
Target . . . .
. . . .

Daily Reward Collection Sheet

Section 3.PDF: page 19

Name . . . .
Date started . . . .
Target . . . .
. . . .

Daily Reward Collection Sheet

Section 3.PDF: page 20

Name . . . .
Date started . . . .
Target . . . .
. . . .

Daily Reward Collection Sheet

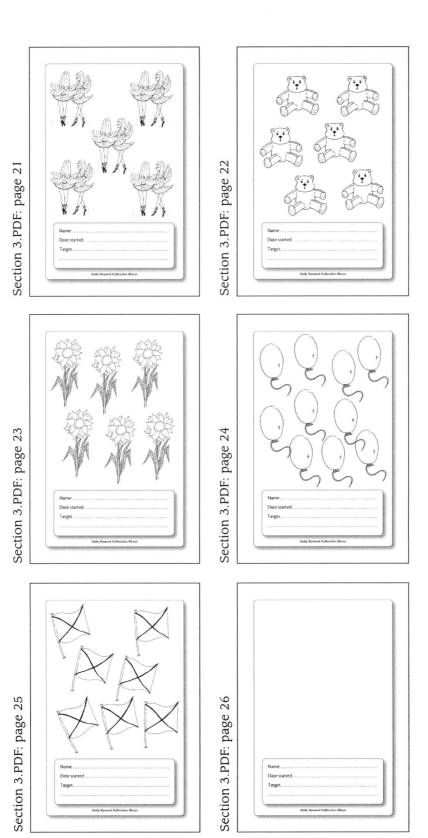

Section 3.PDF: page 21

Section 3.PDF: page 22

Section 3.PDF: page 23

Section 3.PDF: page 24

Section 3.PDF: page 25

Section 3.PDF: page 26

Name ....
Date started ....
Target ....
....

Daily Reward Collection Sheet

Section 4: Weekly Reward Charts

These Weekly Reward Collection Sheets are more suitable for the upper end of Key Stage 1 and lower end of Key Stage 2. They are most appropriate for children who are able to receive daily 'colour in', dot or stickers in recognition of their immediate progress in meeting their agreed target(s), but are able to delay gratification and wait until the end of the week for a reward! Again the target(s) for the week are agreed at the initial meeting with the child and parents/carers and subsequently re-negotiated or adapted as appropriate on a weekly basis.

As with the Daily Reward Collection Sheets, these are also suitable for playtime and classroom use. The children can have access to a sheet of self-adhesive dots or mini-stickers, which they can stick onto the chart, or they may colour in the relevant section, as directed by the teacher. Again, different coloured dots can be used to reward the child at different times in the day in order to allow the teacher to monitor times of the day or specific lessons in which the child experiences most success in meeting their target. This may subsequently help to inform future target setting relevant to the child's needs.

Encouraging the child to place their own 'reward' dots or mini-stickers onto the chart or to colour in the sheet on a daily basis allows active involvement and ongoing recognition of their successes. It also allows the child to reflect upon and reinforce the progress being made in meeting their target over a weekly period. These Reward Sheets provide a full overview of the child's progress over the week.

The completed Reward Sheet can be shown to parents/carers at the end of the week or a copy could be sent home. Alternatively feedback can be given to parents on the telephone, depending on which is most convenient for all those involved.

Examples:

Name .... Mohammed ....

Date started .. 28th March 2005 ....

Target. .... I will ask for help when ....

I don't understand.
....

Name .... Julia ....

Date started .. 28th March 2005 ....

Target. .... I will ask other people first ...

before using their equipment.
....

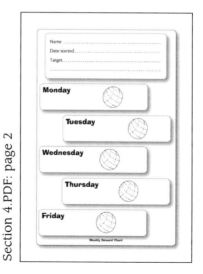

Name...
Date started ....
Target...
....

Monday

Tuesday

Wednesday

Thursday

Friday

Weekly Reward Chart

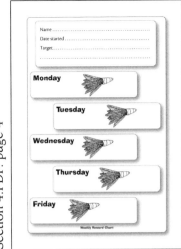

Name...
Date started ....
Target...
....

Monday

Tuesday

Wednesday

Thursday

Friday

Weekly Reward Chart

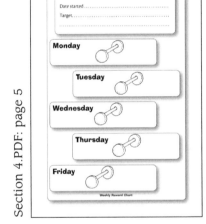

Name...
Date started ....
Target...
....

Monday

Tuesday

Wednesday

Thursday

Friday

Weekly Reward Chart

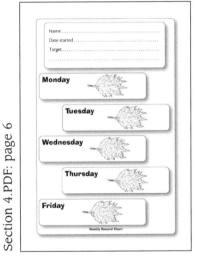

Name...
Date started ....
Target...
....

Monday

Tuesday

Wednesday

Thursday

Friday

Weekly Reward Chart

Name...
Date started ....
Target...
....

Monday

Tuesday

Wednesday

Thursday

Friday

Weekly Reward Chart

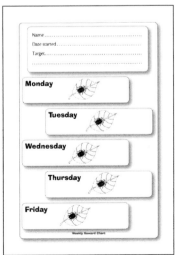

Name...
Date started ....
Target...
....

Monday

Tuesday

Wednesday

Thursday

Friday

Weekly Reward Chart

Name ....
Date started ....
Target ....
....

Monday

Tuesday

Wednesday

Thursday

Friday

Weekly Reward Chart

Name ....
Date started ....
Target ....
....

Monday

Tuesday

Wednesday

Thursday

Friday

Weekly Reward Chart

Name ....
Date started ....
Target ....
....

Monday

Tuesday

Wednesday

Thursday

Friday

Weekly Reward Chart

Name ....
Date started ....
Target ....
....

Monday

Tuesday

Wednesday

Thursday

Friday

Weekly Reward Chart

Name ....
Date started ....
Target ....
....

Monday

Tuesday

Wednesday

Thursday

Friday

Weekly Reward Chart

Name ....
Date started ....
Target ....
....

Monday

Tuesday

Wednesday

Thursday

Friday

Weekly Reward Chart

Name ....
Date started ....
Target ....
....

Monday

Tuesday

Wednesday

Thursday

Friday

Weekly Reward Chart

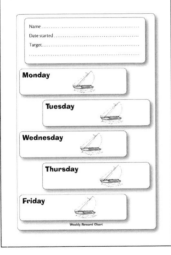

Name ....
Date started ....
Target ....

Monday

Tuesday

Wednesday

Thursday

Friday

Weekly Reward Chart

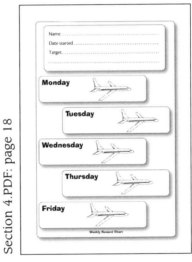

Name ....
Date started ....
Target ....
....

Monday

Tuesday

Wednesday

Thursday

Friday

Weekly Reward Chart

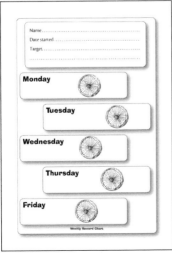

Name ....
Date started ....
Target ....

Monday

Tuesday

Wednesday

Thursday

Friday

Weekly Reward Chart

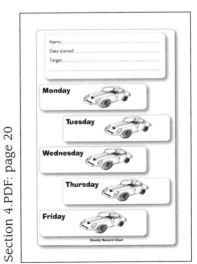

Name ....
Date started ....
Target ....
....

Monday

Tuesday

Wednesday

Thursday

Friday

Weekly Reward Chart

Name ....
Date started ....
Target ....

Monday

Tuesday

Wednesday

Thursday

Friday

Weekly Reward Chart

Name ....
Date started ....
Target. ....
....

Monday

Tuesday

Wednesday

Thursday

Friday

Weekly Reward Chart

Name ....
Date started ....
Target. ....
....

Monday

Tuesday

Wednesday

Thursday

Friday

Weekly Reward Chart

Name ....
Date started ....
Target. ....
....

Monday

Tuesday

Wednesday

Thursday

Friday

Weekly Reward Chart

Name ....
Date started ....
Target. ....
....

Monday

Tuesday

Wednesday

Thursday

Friday

Weekly Reward Chart

Name ....
Date started ....
Target. ....
....

Monday

Tuesday

Wednesday

Thursday

Friday

Weekly Reward Chart

Name ....
Date started ....
Target. ....
....

Monday

Tuesday

Wednesday

Thursday

Friday

Weekly Reward Chart

Section 5: More Specific Weekly Reward Charts

These Weekly Reward Charts differ from Section 4 in that they allow the targets to be broken down into smaller timescales. The children with whom these charts could be used should be able to receive a visual reward in recognition of their progress in meeting their agreed target(s) during different sessions throughout the day, but are possibly more able to wait for their reward until the end of the week. Their targets or a specific target for the week will have been agreed at the initial meeting with the child and parents/carers and subsequently re-negotiated or adapted as appropriate on a weekly basis, or as appropriate to the needs of the child.

The child is awarded a visual reward, for example, mini-sticker, dot or smiley face at the end of each targeted session, which they can collect on their Reward Chart as directed by the teacher. The child can then be rewarded with a special certificate, bookmark or badge reward at the end of the week.

With children in the upper end of Key Stage 2 a scoring system has been found to be very successful, whereby the child and teacher agree a score at the end of each session for the child's effort, concentration and behaviour (related to the specified target). For example, 0 = try harder, 1 = good, 2 = excellent. An appropriate score can then be entered onto the chart at the end of each session and totalled at the end of the week to determine whether the child has met the agreed target score. An appropriate target may be 'Jane will reach a minimum score of 15 points this week for good concentration'. If the agreed minimum score has been achieved the child receives their reward. Involvement of the Special Educational Needs Co-ordinator or head teacher in awarding certificates, bookmarks, badges and any other agreed rewards at the end of the week can be very successful in further motivating the child to achieve their target.

The completed Reward Chart can be shown to parents/carers at the end of the week or a copy could be sent home. Alternatively feedback can be given to parents/carers on the telephone, depending on which is most convenient for all those involved.

Examples:

Name .... Gerard ....

Date started .... 10th October 2005

Target .... I will get my reward if I score 25 dots for good listening.

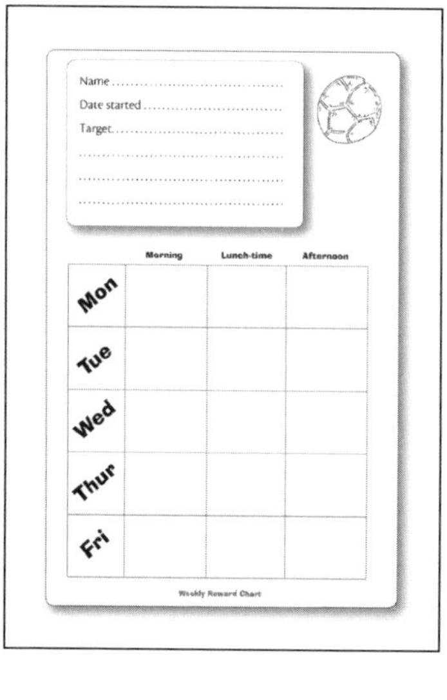
Name
Date started
Target
Morning
Lunch-time
Afternoon
Mon
Tue
Wed
Thur
Fri
Weekly Reward Chart

Section 5.PDF: page 1

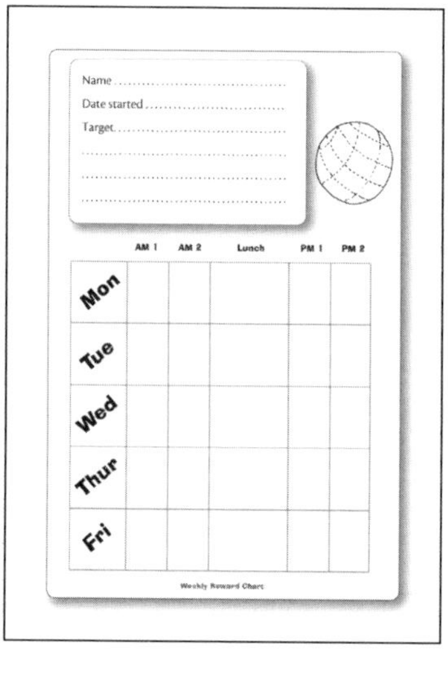
Name
Date started
Target
AM 1
AM 2
Lunch
PM 1
PM 2
Mon
Tue
Wed
Thur
Fri
Weekly Reward Chart

Section 5.PDF: page 2

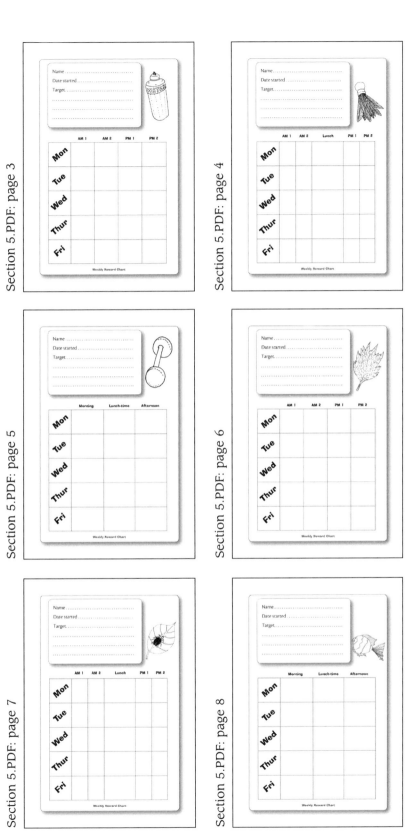

Section 5.PDF: page 3

Name ....
Date started ....
Target. ....
....
....
....

	AM 1	AM 2	PM 1	PM 2
Mon				
Tue				
Wed				
Thur				
Fri				

Weekly Reward Chart

Section 5.PDF: page 4

Name ....
Date started ....
Target. ....
....
....
....

	AM 1	AM 2	Lunch	PM 1	PM 2
Mon					
Tue					
Wed					
Thur					
Fri					

Weekly Reward Chart

Section 5.PDF: page 5

Name ....
Date started ....
Target. ....
....
....
....

	Morning	Lunch-time	Afternoon
Mon			
Tue			
Wed			
Thur			
Fri			

Weekly Reward Chart

Section 5.PDF: page 6

Name ....
Date started ....
Target. ....
....
....
....

	AM 1	AM 2	PM 1	PM 2
Mon				
Tue				
Wed				
Thur				
Fri				

Weekly Reward Chart

Section 5.PDF: page 7

Name ....
Date started ....
Target. ....
....
....
....

	AM 1	AM 2	Lunch	PM 1	PM 2
Mon					
Tue					
Wed					
Thur					
Fri					

Weekly Reward Chart

Section 5.PDF: page 8

Name ....
Date started ....
Target. ....
....
....
....

	Morning	Lunch-time	Afternoon
Mon			
Tue			
Wed			
Thur			
Fri			

Weekly Reward Chart

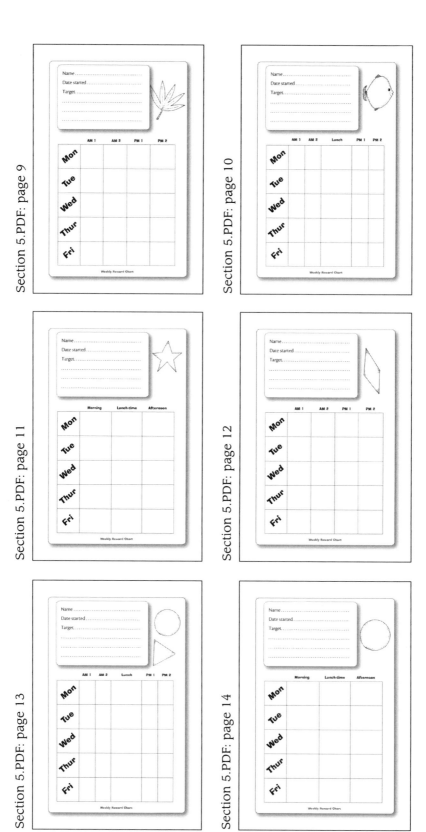

Section 5.PDF: page 9

Section 5.PDF: page 11

Section 5.PDF: page 13

Section 5.PDF: page 10

Section 5.PDF: page 12

Section 5.PDF: page 14

42

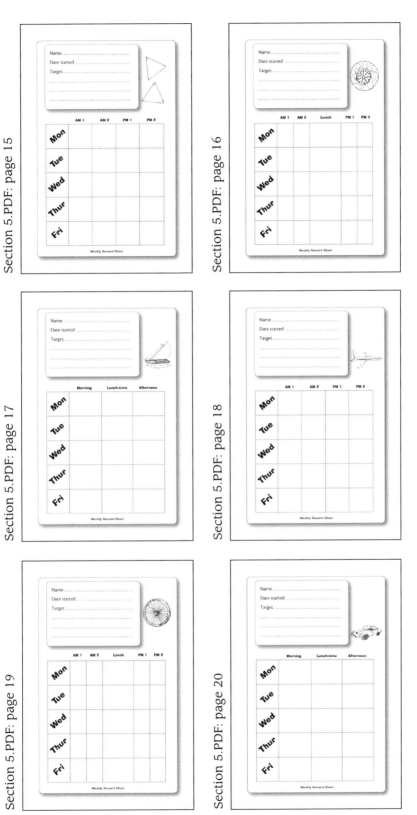

Section 5.PDF: page 15

Section 5.PDF: page 16

Section 5.PDF: page 17

Section 5.PDF: page 18

Section 5.PDF: page 19

Section 5.PDF: page 20

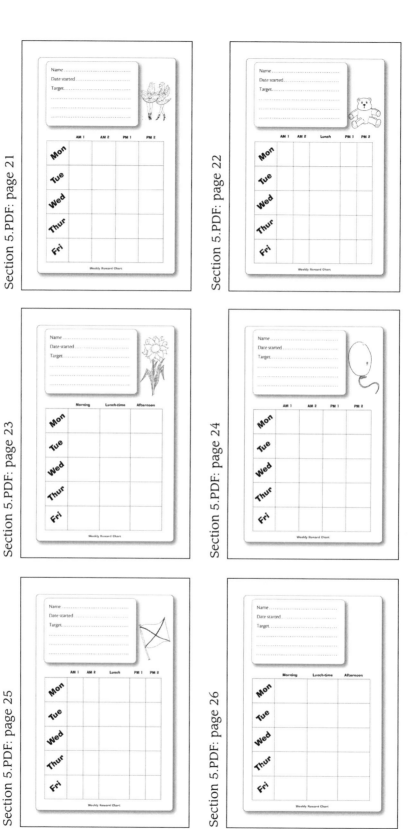

Section 5.PDF: page 21

Section 5.PDF: page 22

Section 5.PDF: page 23

Section 5.PDF: page 24

Section 5.PDF: page 25

Section 5.PDF: page 26

Section 6: Playtime Reward Charts

These Playtime Reward Charts can also be stored in an A4 Target Book or folder. They are designed to specifically promote and reward appropriate behaviour and social skills at playtimes and lunchtimes, and are most appropriate for use with children at the upper end of Key Stage 1 and at Key Stage 2. Again, the targets and any supporting programme of social skills training, emotional literacy, etc., will have been agreed at the initial meeting between the teacher, parents/carers and child.

Children are awarded an immediate visual reward, for example, mini-sticker, dot or smiley face, which they can collect on the Playtime Reward Chart as directed by the teacher or lunchtime supervisor upon meeting the desired target. Children can then be rewarded with a special sticker, certificate or bookmark reward at the end of each day or week, as appropriate. It may be helpful to set a specific target for the whole week if the latter approach is adopted, for example, 'Sara will receive her bookmark reward if she has a minimum of 8 "good" playtimes this week.'

When making use of these Playtime Reward Charts, or any behaviour modification at playtimes and lunchtimes, it is essential to ensure that all staff and lunchtime supervisors are aware of the programme in place for the child, and understand how they can support the child in meeting their target(s). In our experience, this can be best achieved at a team meeting with the relevant staff and (SENCO). This allows for a consistent approach, encourages feedback and liaison between staff, and ensures that the child is given the best possible chance to succeed.

The completed Playtime Reward Chart can be shown to parents/carers at the end of the week or a copy could be sent home. Alternatively feedback can be given to parents/carers on the telephone, depending on which is most convenient for all those involved.

Example:

Name .Josh.................................

Date started....28th March 2005..

Target. I will ask for help

.... when I get angry.

....

....

Name .Lucy.................................

Date started...10th May 2005.....

Target. I will line up when the

.... whistle blows and stand

.... quietly.

....

Name ....
Date started ....
Target ....
....
....

	Morning playtime	Lunch time	Afternoon playtime
Mon			
Tue			
Wed			
Thur			
Fri			

Playtime Reward Chart

Name ....
Date started ....
Target ....
....
....

	Morning playtime	Lunch time	Afternoon playtime
Mon			
Tue			
Wed			
Thur			
Fri			

Playtime Reward Chart

Name ....
Date started ....
Target ....
....
....

	Morning playtime	Lunch time	Afternoon playtime
Mon			
Tue			
Wed			
Thur			
Fri			

Playtime Reward Chart

Name ....
Date started ....
Target ....
....
....

	Morning playtime	Lunch time	Afternoon playtime
Mon			
Tue			
Wed			
Thur			
Fri			

Playtime Reward Chart

Name ....
Date started ....
Target ....
....
....

	Morning playtime	Lunch time	Afternoon playtime
Mon			
Tue			
Wed			
Thur			
Fri			

Playtime Reward Chart

Name ....
Date started ....
Target ....
....
....

	Morning playtime	Lunch time	Afternoon playtime
Mon			
Tue			
Wed			
Thur			
Fri			

Playtime Reward Chart

Section 6.PDF: page 9

Section 6.PDF: page 10

Section 6.PDF: page 11

Section 6.PDF: page 12

Section 6.PDF: page 13

Section 5.PDF: page 14

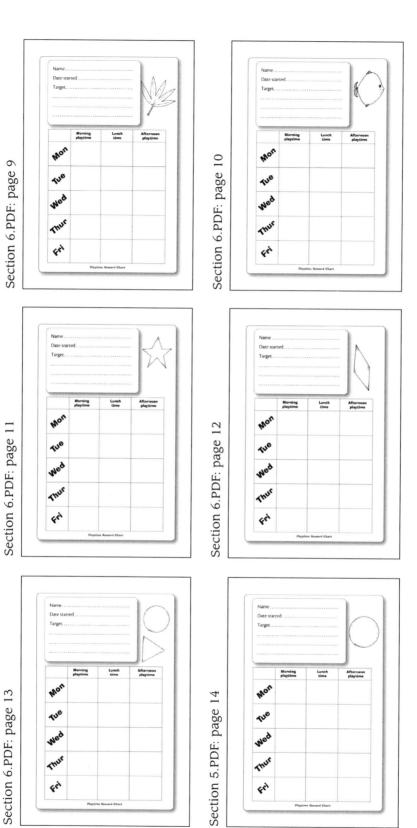

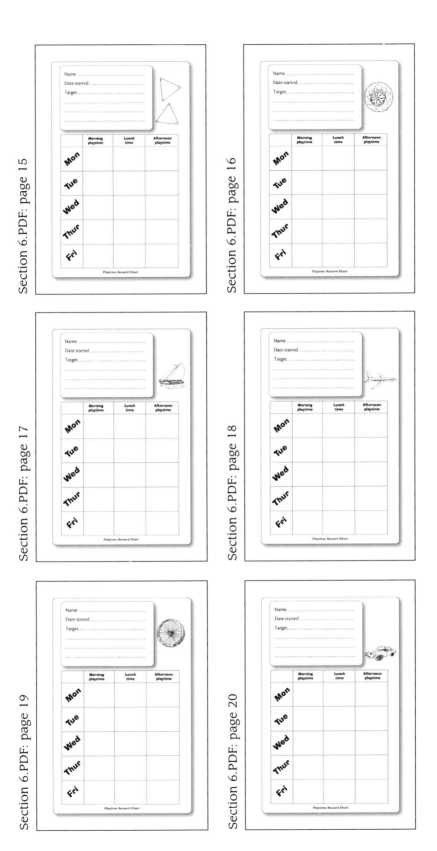

Section 6.PDF: page 15

Section 6.PDF: page 16

Section 6.PDF: page 17

Section 6.PDF: page 18

Section 6.PDF: page 19

Section 6.PDF: page 20

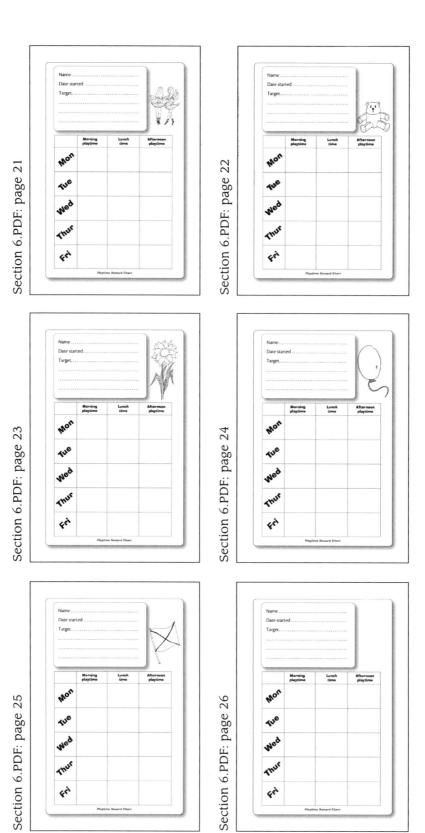

Section 6.PDF: page 21

Name ....
Date started ....
Target..............................
....
....
....

	Morning playtime	Lunch time	Afternoon playtime
Mon			
Tue			
Wed			
Thur			
Fri			

Playtime Reward Chart

Section 6.PDF: page 22

Name ....
Date started ....
Target..............................
....
....
....

	Morning playtime	Lunch time	Afternoon playtime
Mon			
Tue			
Wed			
Thur			
Fri			

Playtime Reward Chart

Section 6.PDF: page 23

Name ....
Date started ....
Target..............................
....
....
....

	Morning playtime	Lunch time	Afternoon playtime
Mon			
Tue			
Wed			
Thur			
Fri			

Playtime Reward Chart

Section 6.PDF: page 24

Name ....
Date started ....
Target..............................
....
....
....

	Morning playtime	Lunch time	Afternoon playtime
Mon			
Tue			
Wed			
Thur			
Fri			

Playtime Reward Chart

Section 6.PDF: page 25

Name ....
Date started ....
Target..............................
....
....
....

	Morning playtime	Lunch time	Afternoon playtime
Mon			
Tue			
Wed			
Thur			
Fri			

Playtime Reward Chart

Section 6.PDF: page 26

Name ....
Date started ....
Target..............................
....
....
....

	Morning playtime	Lunch time	Afternoon playtime
Mon			
Tue			
Wed			
Thur			
Fri			

Playtime Reward Chart

Section 7: Reward Charts for School and Home Comments

The Reward Charts included in this section follow the same principles as the Playtime and Weekly Reward Charts (refer to Sections 5 and 6). However, in addition to the procedures described for other Reward Charts, teachers and parents/carers are also requested to comment positively on the child's progress in meeting the agreed target(s). These comments can be made on a daily or weekly basis, depending on the decision made at the initial meeting between the teacher, parents/carers and child. Formats are included for selection of the most appropriate method, depending on the need for daily or weekly monitoring and the regularity of feedback required between home and school.

At the end of each day or week, as appropriate, the teacher should make a comment on the child's progress towards meeting their target(s) in the space provided on the Reward Chart for 'School comments'. The completed Reward Chart can then be shown to parents/carers, or a copy could be sent home in order to request parents to make a positive comment in the space allocated.

The use of these Reward Charts will ensure ongoing liaison between home and school using a united approach that rewards their achievements and successes in a positive way.

Examples:

Name Josh ....

Date started ... 28th March 2005 ...

Target. I ask for help when ....

.... I get angry. ....

....

....

Name Lucy ....

Date started ... 10th May 2005 ....

Target. I will line up when the ....

.... whistle blows and stand ....

.... quietly. ....

....

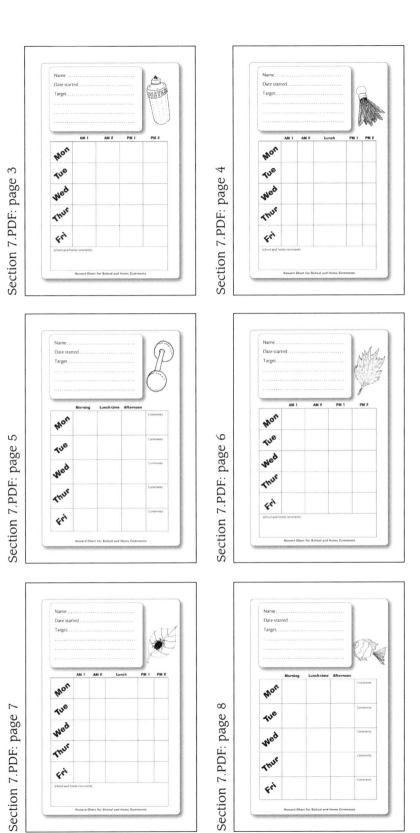

Section 7.PDF: page 3

Section 7.PDF: page 4

Section 7.PDF: page 5

Section 7.PDF: page 6

Section 7.PDF: page 7

Section 7.PDF: page 8

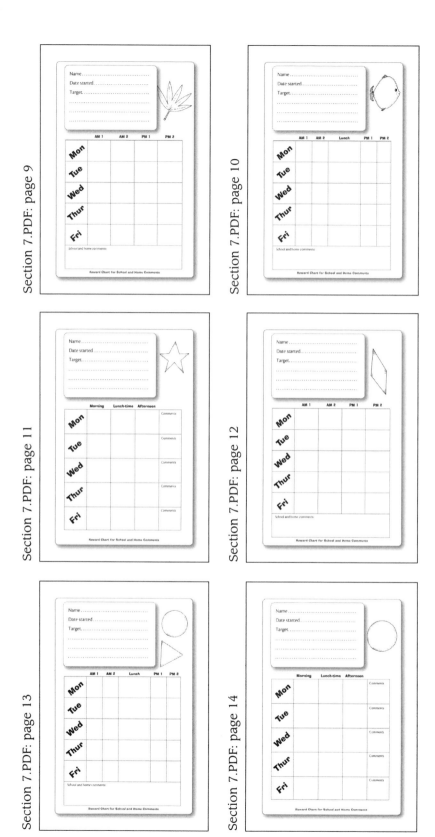

Section 7.PDF: page 9

Section 7.PDF: page 10

Section 7.PDF: page 11

Section 7.PDF: page 12

Section 7.PDF: page 13

Section 7.PDF: page 14

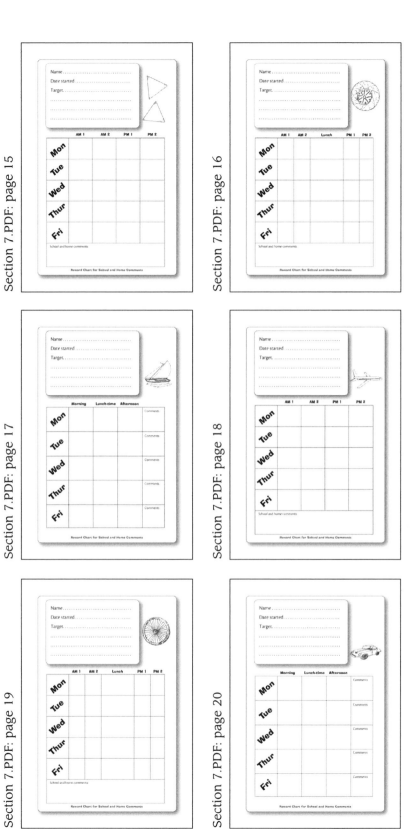

Section 7.PDF: page 15

Section 7.PDF: page 16

Section 7.PDF: page 17

Section 7.PDF: page 18

Section 7.PDF: page 19

Section 7.PDF: page 20

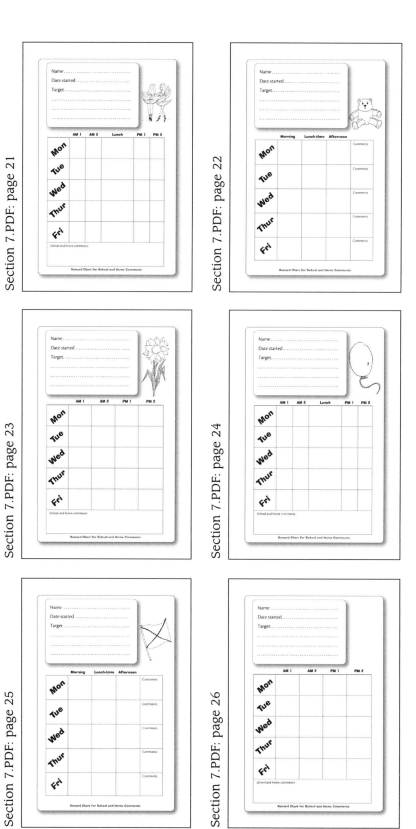

Section 7.PDF: page 21

Section 7.PDF: page 22

Section 7.PDF: page 23

Section 7.PDF: page 24

Section 7.PDF: page 25

Section 7.PDF: page 26

56

Section 8: Sticker Sheets

For younger children, in particular, we have found the use of sticker rewards to be very successful in providing the child with an instant feeling of success which allows for continual reinforcement of the set target and desired behaviours. Every time the teacher observes the child 'being good' or meeting the set target, the child can be given an immediate sticker reward. This promotes a positive approach, which can be very affirming for the child and encourages further reinforcement of positive behaviours and learning attitudes.

These sticker rewards can be used to motivate individual children to meet an agreed target for their behaviour or learning in a variety of contexts. They can also be very successful in rewarding groups of children in identified target areas, for example, by setting a group target to use capital letters and full stops correctly in their writing, and providing a sticker reward for each child who achieves this in the lesson.

The sticker rewards can be stuck onto the child's work in order to value their achievements or learning behaviours, or alternatively may be worn by the child in order to share and celebrate their successes with peers and parents/carers. Children may feel a real sense of pride in wearing a sticker reward and this can be inspiring and motivational for them.

The sticker sheets provided in this section are designed to be printed onto blank A4 self-adhesive sticker sheets, which may be purchased from a good educational supplier or stationer. This can be achieved by photocopying the sticker sheet designs, and using the manual paper-feed tray of the photocopier through which to feed the self-adhesive sheets. This will then produce a sheet of stickers of the chosen design. The stickers will then need to be cut out by the teacher in order to produce individual sticker rewards.

These sticker sheets may also be used to award to children who are using the Daily or Weekly Reward Charts from this resource bank. In order to use them for this purpose, the sticker sheets will need to be reduced on the photocopier to an appropriate size prior to photocopying onto the self-adhesive sticker sheets.

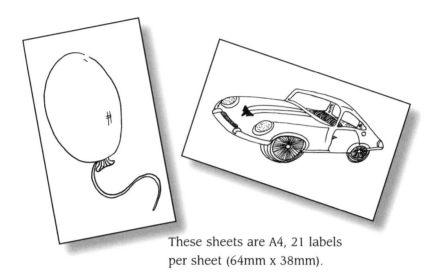

These sheets are A4, 21 labels per sheet (64mm x 38mm).

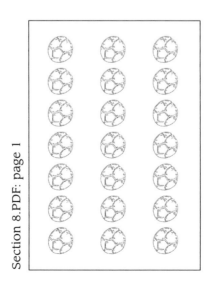

Section 8.PDF: page 1

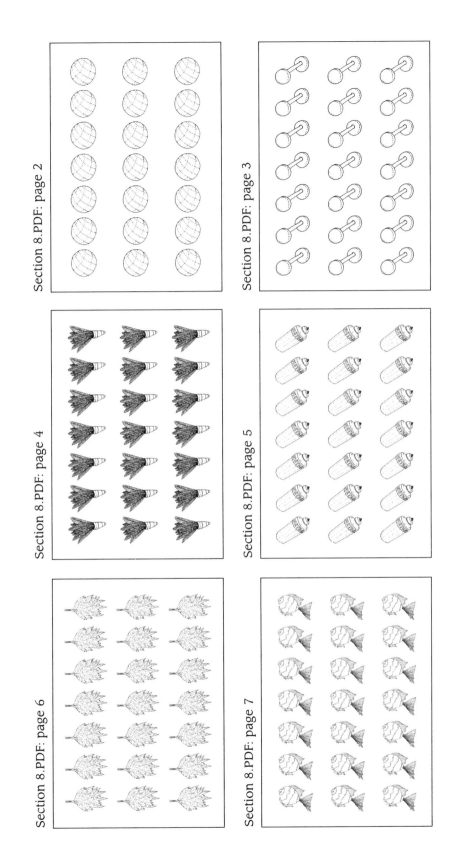

Section 8.PDF: page 2

Section 8.PDF: page 3

Section 8.PDF: page 4

Section 8.PDF: page 5

Section 8.PDF: page 6

Section 8.PDF: page 7

59

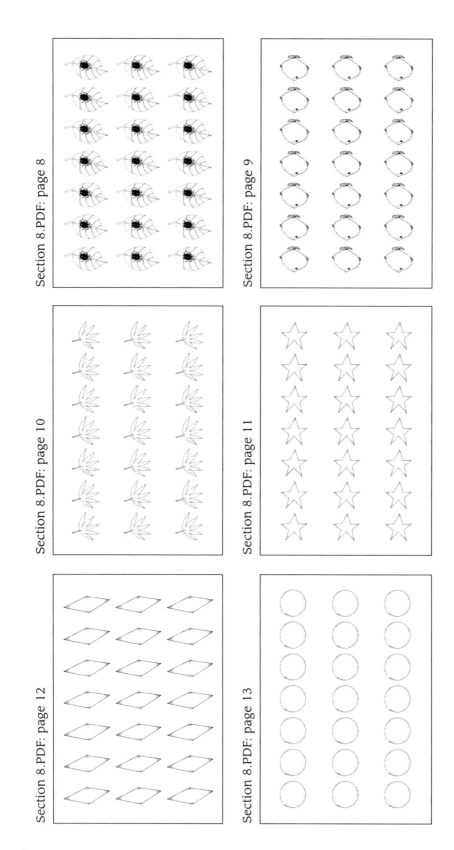

Section 8.PDF: page 8

Section 8.PDF: page 9

Section 8.PDF: page 10

Section 8.PDF: page 11

Section 8.PDF: page 12

Section 8.PDF: page 13

60

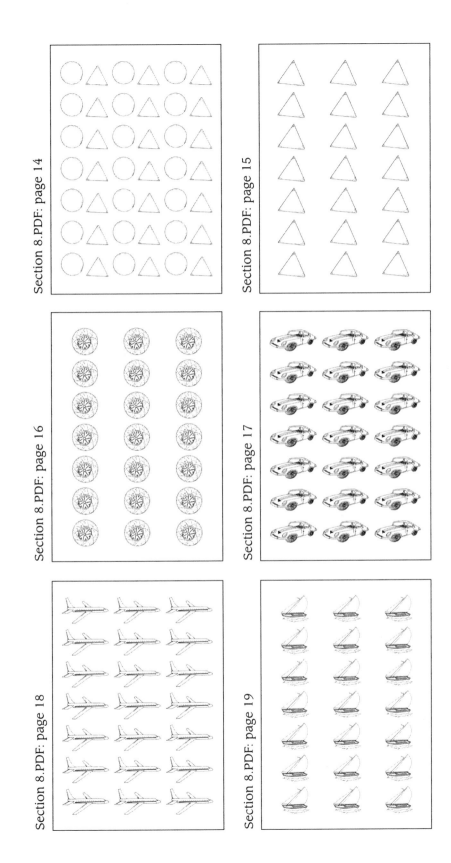

Section 8.PDF: page 14

Section 8.PDF: page 15

Section 8.PDF: page 16

Section 8.PDF: page 17

Section 8.PDF: page 18

Section 8.PDF: page 19

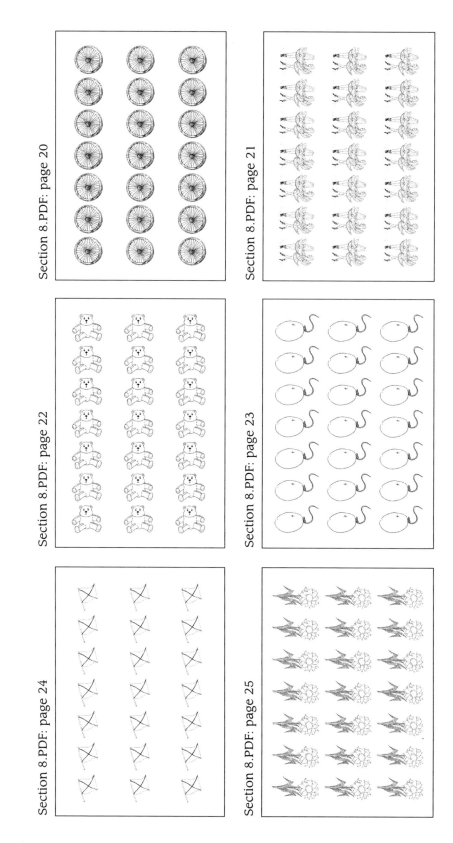

Section 8.PDF: page 20

Section 8.PDF: page 21

Section 8.PDF: page 22

Section 8.PDF: page 23

Section 8.PDF: page 24

Section 8.PDF: page 25

Section 9: Certificates for School and Home

This section of the resource bank provides teachers with a variety of achievement certificates, which may be used to reward children's behaviour and learning. They use positive comments and illustrations from a selection of the Rewards Sheets and Charts provided in the earlier sections.

The use of reward certificates in primary schools is now a well-established means of valuing children's efforts and progress. They can be used to reward children when they reach their targets and on successful completion of their Reward Sheets and Charts. The certificates may also be used as a valuable resource throughout the school in celebrating a variety of different types of children's progress, for example, in a weekly Achievement Assembly, where two children are nominated from each class to receive a certificate for their own personal successes.

To prepare these certificates for use, the teacher will need to print the selected certificate(s) onto thin A4 card. Different coloured card could be used to add variety to these resources and further develop the children's enjoyment in receiving them. To add further decoration and value to this reward the teacher or child may also colour in the illustrations on the certificates. The certificates can finally be completed with the child's name, the reason for receiving the certificate, the teacher's signature and date.

In addition to the certificates provided in this section, teachers, parents/carers and children may choose to make use of the blank certificate formats. They may use these to develop their own personalised reward certificates, which could be designed using illustrations relevant to the different children's interests, or by using printed stickers. Children may also enjoy designing their own certificates using these formats and awarding them to their peers in recognition of each other's achievements and successes.

If you want more certificates, the publication *Celebrations* (Robinson and Maines 1995) has over 190 certificates.

This has been awarded to

Name.....................................
Signed........................Date..............

For
....
....

Well Done!

This has been awarded to

Name.....................................
Signed........................Date..............

For
....
....

Well Done!

This has been awarded to

Name ....
Signed .... Date ....

For

....
....

Well Done!

This has been awarded to

Name ....
Signed .... Date ....

For

....
....

Well Done!

This has been awarded to

Name ....
Signed .... Date ....

For

....
....

Well Done!

This has been awarded to

Name ....
Signed .... Date ....

For

....
....

Well Done!

This has been awarded to

Name ....
Signed .... Date ....

For

....
....

Well Done!

This has been awarded to

Name ....
Signed .... Date ....

For

....
....

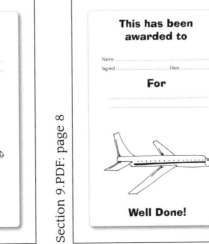

Well Done!

**This has been
awarded to**

Name ....
Signed ....Date ....

For

....
....

Well Done!

**This has been
awarded to**

Name ....
Signed ....Date ....

For

....
....

Well Done!

**This has been
awarded to**

Name ....
Signed ....Date ....

For

....
....

Well Done!

**This has been
awarded to**

Name ....
Signed ....Date ....

For

....
....

Well Done!

**This has been
awarded to**

Name ....
Signed ....Date ....

For

....
....

Well Done!

**This has been
awarded to**

Name ....
Signed ....Date ....

For

....
....

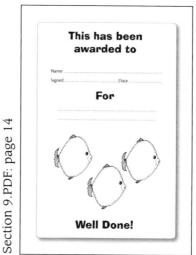

Well Done!

This has been awarded to

Name ....
Signed .... Date ....

For

....
....

Well Done!

This has been awarded to

Name ....
Signed .... Date ....

For

....
....

Well Done!

This has been awarded to

Name ....
Signed .... Date ....

For

....
....

Well Done!

This has been awarded to

Name ....
Signed .... Date ....

For

....
....

Well Done!

This has been awarded to

Name ....
Signed .... Date ....

For

....
....

Well Done!

This has been awarded to

Name ....
Signed .... Date ....

For

....
....

Well Done!

This has been awarded to

Name ....

Signed .... Date ....

For

....

....

Well Done!

This has been awarded to

Name ....

Signed .... Date ....

For

....

....

Well Done!

This has been awarded to

Name ....

Signed .... Date ....

For

....

....

Well Done!

This has been awarded to

Name ....

Signed .... Date ....

For

....

....

Well Done!

This has been awarded to

Name ....

Signed .... Date ....

For

....

....

Well Done!

This has been awarded to

Name ....

Signed .... Date ....

For

....

....

Well Done!

Section 10: Reward Badges

The Reward Badges provided in this section may be used in schools as an additional, special reward for children who may have been particularly successful in reaching their targets for behaviour or learning.

Children across the primary age range have been found to respond very favourably when receiving a badge for their personal achievements, as this type of reward can be unusual and fun. It is also a valuable method of sharing and celebrating their own successes with their peers, other members of staff and parents/carers, because people can see a special reward badge and make favourable comments.

We would recommend that these badges are reserved for particularly special achievements in order to provide children with a higher level of reward to aim for, and to give extra praise and recognition when they have made more noticeable effort or progress. This also enables them to build up and develop their achievement of different types of rewards, which may be dependent on the relative success that they have in meeting their targets, using a progressive approach.

In order to prepare these Reward Badges, the teacher will need to print the sheets provided in this section onto thin A4 card. Coloured card may also be used to add variety to the reward badges, or the child or teacher can colour them in to further improve their presentation and attractiveness. These badges may be laminated or covered in sticky back plastic to increase their durability and this will also give them a shiny, polished finished. Each individual Reward Badge will then need to be carefully cut out. Finally, a safety pin should be secured to the reverse side of the badge using sticky tape or a low melt glue gun, being careful to ensure that the safety pin is left free to open and close.

The Reward Badge is then ready for the child to wear with pride!

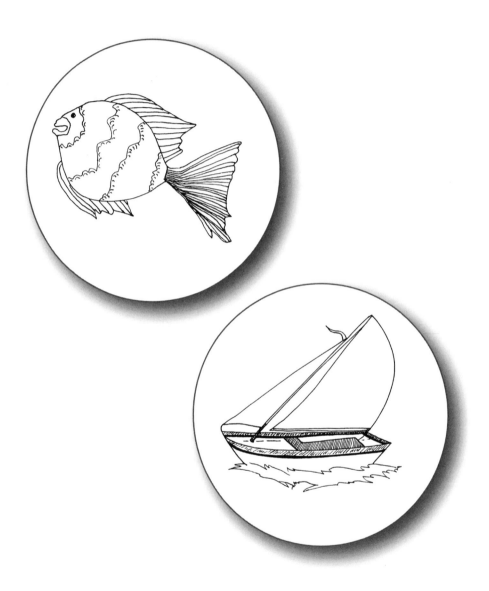

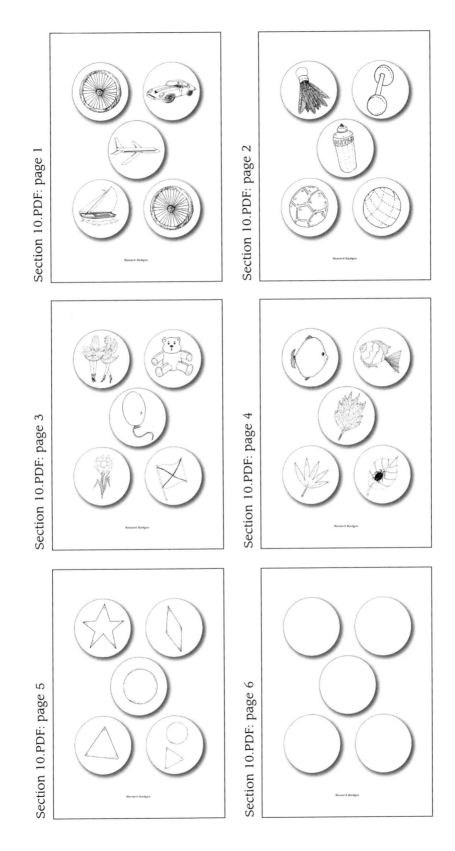

Section 10.PDF: page 1

Section 10.PDF: page 2

Section 10.PDF: page 3

Section 10.PDF: page 4

Section 10.PDF: page 5

Section 10.PDF: page 6

Section 11: Bookmark Rewards

This section provides teachers with a variety of Bookmark Rewards, which use similar illustrations to a selection of the Rewards Sheets and Charts provided in the earlier sections of this resource bank. They are designed to complement the other resources provided in this pack, but may also be used successfully as a 'stand alone' resource to award to children wherever the teacher may find them useful, for example, as a special library award or for members of a reading club.

These Bookmark Rewards can be used to award children with a special and useful reward for their personal achievements. We have found that children particularly enjoy receiving these bookmarks because they are seen as practical and fun. They can be highly motivating for children of all ages, but particularly with older children for whom the novelty of stickers and certificates may have worn off through their repeated use during the earlier years of school. Older children also perceive these bookmarks to be more rewarding due to their increased levels of maturity and the subsequent need for more age-appropriate reward systems. These Bookmark Rewards have been welcomed by teachers, and have provided them with further incentives to successfully motivate children.

When preparing these Bookmark Rewards, teachers will need to print the chosen designs onto A4 sized thin card. Alternatively teachers, parents/carers or children may design their own bookmarks using the blank formats. Different coloured card may be used to provide an interesting variety of bookmarks and to add value and interest to them. The individual bookmarks can then be cut out so that they are ready for awarding to the child on successful completion of their Reward Sheets or Charts.

The teacher can complete the relevant spaces on the bookmark reward by writing the child's name, the date and by signing the bookmark to provide additional authorisation of the child' success. The teacher or child may also wish to colour the illustration on the bookmark in order to make it more decorative and colourful.

Finally, the completed bookmark reward could be laminated or covered with sticky back plastic in order to make it into a more permanent, practical reward which the child can then use as a bookmark in their reading book or target book.

Section 11.PDF: page 1

Section 11.PDF: page 2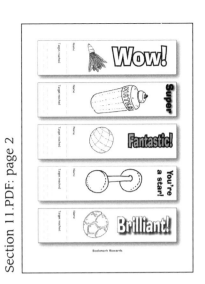

Section 11.PDF: page 3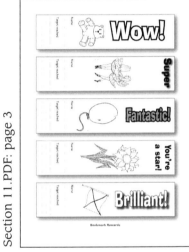

Section 11.PDF: page 4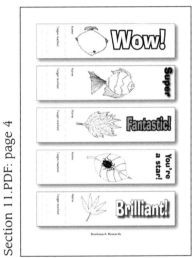

Section 11.PDF: page 5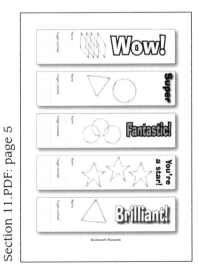

Section 11.PDF: page 6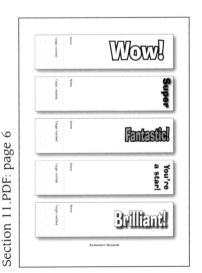

Section 12: Achievement Card

This section of the resource bank comprises five different styles of Achievement Cards. These provide attractive resources which enable personalised target setting, immediate rewards and a quick visual system to monitor individual children's progress against their agreed targets.

As with all good target setting practice, the targets set for children should be agreed between the teacher, child and parents/carers in order to ensure a consistent approach, with ownership by the child. The targets should be worded positively so that the child knows exactly what behaviours or learning is expected of them. They should also be specific, measurable, achievable, realistic and within an agreed time limit, for example, 'I will sit on the carpet with my legs crossed and hands in my lap, looking at the teacher'. A review date should then be arranged.

The teacher, parent/carer or child may select one front cover design from the chosen style of Achievement Card and print this onto thin A4 card. Coloured card may be used, if required. The corresponding Reward Collection inside sheet will then need to be printed back to back onto the same piece of card, ensuring that the text is the same way up on both sides. The Achievement Card is then ready to be folded in half to make it into A5 size, with the title and illustrated design on the front. The child's name and date of starting can then be written onto the front of the Achievement Card. The child may also choose to personalise their card by colouring in the illustration.

The child's agreed targets should be written into the spaces provided inside the Achievement Card. Each time the child is then observed reaching one of their targets, an agreed reward may be given (mini-sticker, dot, smiley face or point).

An agreed time limit will need to be decided, and at the end of this period the total number of rewards collected for each target may be counted up and entered into the spaces provided. The teacher may then use this to monitor the child's progress in reaching their targets, which could be used to inform future target setting in a cyclical way.

The blank format at the end of the section may be used if teachers, parents/ carers or children wish to design their own personalised front covers for their Achievement Card and may assist children in feeling an increased level of ownership. The relevant Reward Collection inside sheets will then need to be used from those provided in this section of the resource bank.

Example:

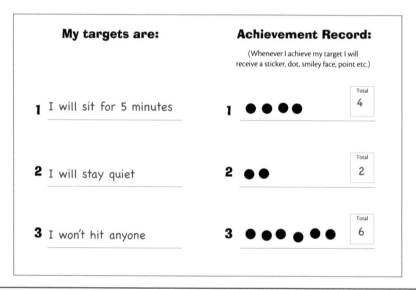

My targets are:

Achievement Record:

(Whenever I achieve my target I will receive a sticker, dot, smiley face, point etc.)

1 I will sit for 5 minutes   1 ● ● ●●   Total **4**

2 I will stay quiet   **2** ●●   Total **2**

3 I won't hit anyone   **3** ●●● ● ●●   Total **6**

Section 12.PDF: page 1

Achievement Card

Name ....
Date started ....
Date completed ....

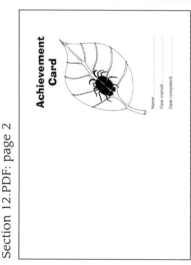

Section 12.PDF: page 2

Achievement Card

Name ....
Date started ....
Date completed ....

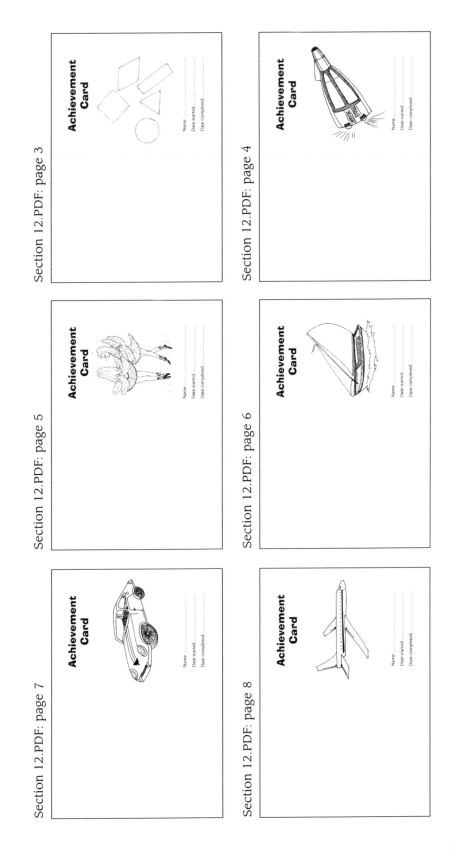

Section 12.PDF: page 3

Achievement Card

Name....................
Date started..............
Date completed..............

Section 12.PDF: page 4

Achievement Card

Name....................
Date started..............
Date completed..............

Section 12.PDF: page 5

Achievement Card

Name....................
Date started..............
Date completed..............

Section 12.PDF: page 6

Achievement Card

Name....................
Date started..............
Date completed..............

Section 12.PDF: page 7

Achievement Card

Name....................
Date started..............
Date completed..............

Section 12.PDF: page 8

Achievement Card

Name....................
Date started..............
Date completed..............

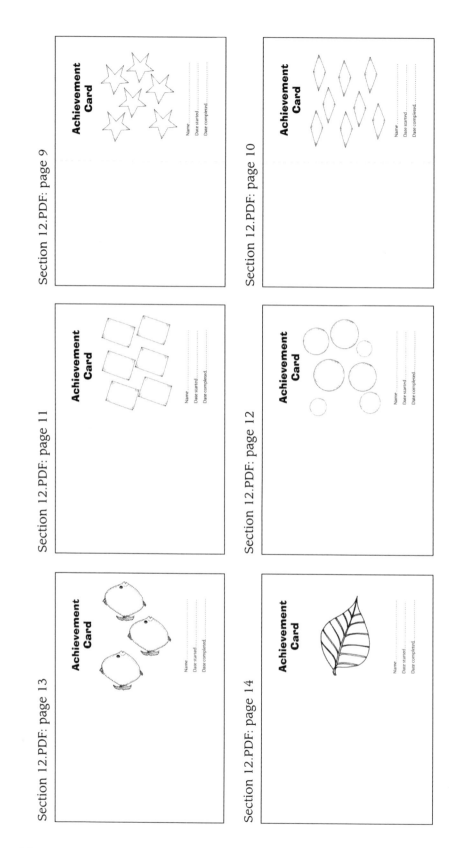

Section 12.PDF: page 9

Section 12.PDF: page 10

Section 12.PDF: page 11

Section 12.PDF: page 12

Section 12.PDF: page 13

Section 12.PDF: page 14

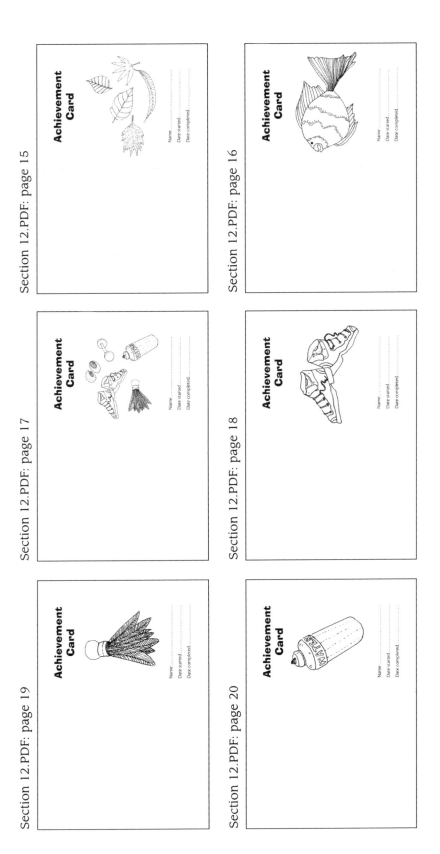

Section 12.PDF: page 15

Section 12.PDF: page 16

Section 12.PDF: page 17

Section 12.PDF: page 18

Section 12.PDF: page 19

Section 12.PDF: page 20

Achievement Card

Name ....
Date started ....
Date completed. ....

Section 12.PDF: page 21

Achievement Card

Name ....
Date started ....
Date completed ....

Section 12.PDF: page 21

Achievement Card

Name ....
Date started ....
Date completed ....

Section 12.PDF: page 23

Achievement Card

Name ....
Date started ....
Date completed ....

Section 12.PDF: page 24

Achievement Card

Name ....
Date started ....
Date completed ....

Section 12.PDF: page 25

Achievement Card

Name ....
Date started ....
Date completed ....

Section 12.PDF: page 26

My targets are:

Achievement Record:
(Whenever I achieve my target I will receive a sticker, dot, smiley face, point etc.)

1 _____   1   Total

2 _____   2   Total

3 _____   3   Total